Having an Eye Test

Vic Parker

Heinemann Library
Chicago, Illinois

www.heinemannraintree.com
Visit our website to find out more information about Heinemann-Raintree books.

To order:
☎ Phone 888-454-2279
⌨ Visit www.heinemannraintree.com to browse our catalog and order online.

Edited by Dan Nunn, Rebecca Rissman, and Sian Smith
Designed by Joanna Hinton-Malivoire
Picture research by Elizabeth Alexander
Originated by Capstone Global Library Ltd
Printed in the United States of America by
    Worzalla Publishing.

15 14 13 12 11 10
10 9 8 7 6 5 4 3 2 1

Library of Congress Cataloging-in-Publication Data
Parker, Victoria.
  Having an eye test / Vic Parker.
    p. cm.—(Growing up)
  Includes bibliographical references and index.
  ISBN 978-1-4329-4798-9 (hc)—ISBN 978-1-4329-4808-5
(pb) 1. Eye—Examination—Juvenile literature. I. Title.
  RE75.P35 2011
  617.7'15—dc22   2010024192

Acknowledgments
We would like to thank the following for permission to reproduce photographs: Alamy pp. 10 (© amana images inc.), 12, 14, 16, 23 glossary expert (© Image Source), 18 (© Sally and Richard Greenhill); Corbis pp. 5 (© Bernd Vogel), 17 (© JLP/Jose L. Pelaez), 21 (© Pauline St. Denis); Getty Images p. 8 (altrendo images/ Stockbyte); iStockphoto pp. 4 (© Rob Friedman), 11 (© Izabela Habur); Photolibrary pp. 6 (Leah Warkentin/ Design Pics Inc), 9, 23 glossary optician (UpperCut Images); Science Photo Library pp. 20, 23 glossary eye drops (David Hay Jones), 19, 23 glossary eye patch (Mark Clarke); Shutterstock pp. 7 (© Elena Elisseeva), 13, 23 glossary lenses (© GWImages), 15 (© lightpoet).

Front cover photograph of a boy looking at eye examination equipment reproduced with permission of Alamy (© Blend Images). Back cover photographs of an optician reproduced with permission of iStockphoto (© Izabela Habur), and lenses reproduced with permission of Shutterstock (© GWImages).

We would like to thank Matthew Siegel for his invaluable help in the preparation of this book.

Every effort has been made to contact copyright holders of material reproduced in this book. Any omissions will be rectified in subsequent printings if notice is given to the publisher.

Disclaimer
All the Internet addresses (URLs) given in this book were valid at the time of going to press. However, due to the dynamic nature of the Internet, some addresses may have changed or ceased to exist since publication. While the author and publisher regret any inconvenience this may cause readers, no responsibility for any such changes can be accepted by either the author or the publisher.

Contents

Some words are shown in bold, **like this**.
You can find them in the glossary on page 23.

What Is an Eye Test?

You see things with your eyes.

An eye test is a check to see that both your eyes are working properly.

An eye test will make sure you can see things that are close up.

It will also make sure you can see things that are far away.

Why Might I Have an Eye Test?

You might have an eye test because you have reached a certain age.

Most children have eye tests during their first year in school.

Sometimes your teacher, parent, or doctor might think you have a problem with your sight.

You may have an eye test then, too.

Where Will It Happen?

Some eye tests are done at school.

The eye test might happen in the school nurse's room or in an empty classroom.

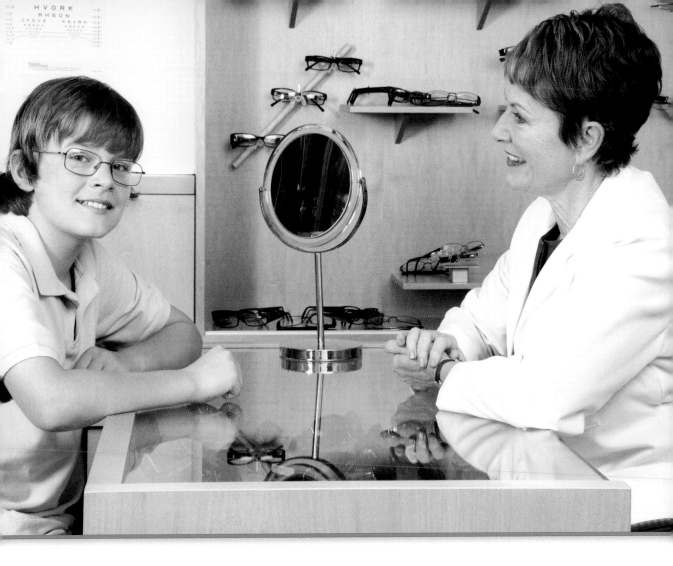

Many people have their eyes tested
in an eyeglass store by a person called
an **optometrist**.

You can also buy glasses from your
optometrist.

Who Will I Meet?

Sometimes an eye **expert** will come into school to do eye tests.

Sometimes eye tests at school are done by the school nurse.

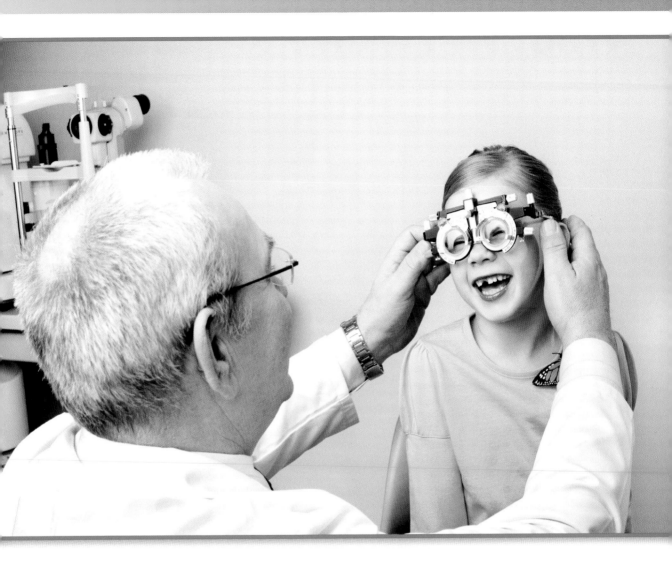

If you go to a store, your eye test will be done by an **optometrist**.

Optometrists are eye experts, too.

What Will I Have to Do?

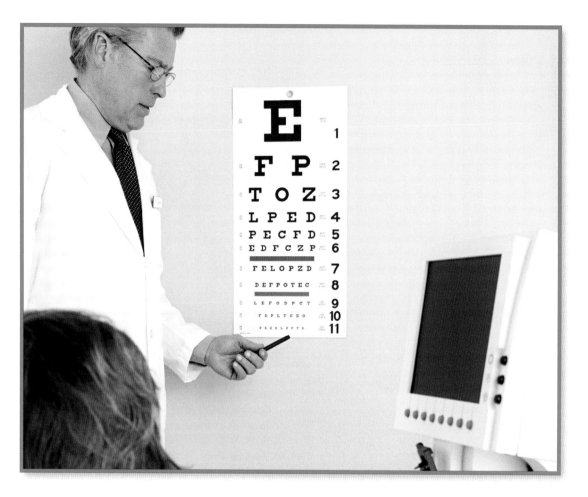

With one eye covered, you will look at a chart with letters on it and say what you can see.

Then you will do it again with the other eye covered.

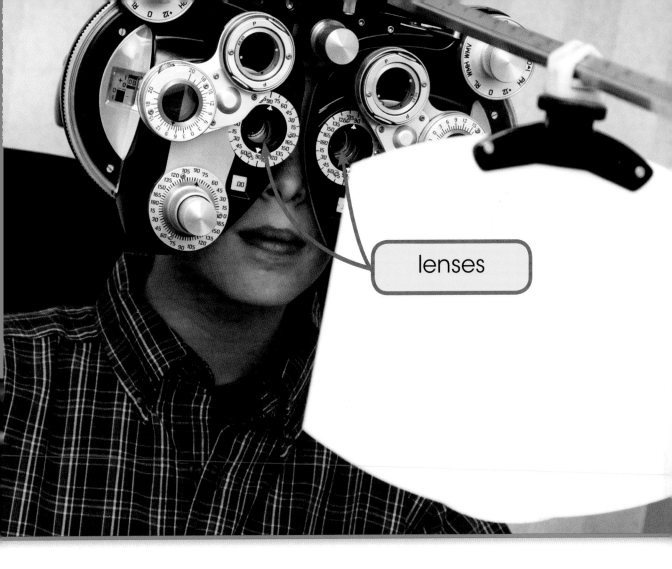

lenses

You may have to look at a picture through some special equipment.

The eye **expert** will change **lenses** in the equipment and ask you if the picture is clearer or more blurry.

What Other Equipment Might I See?

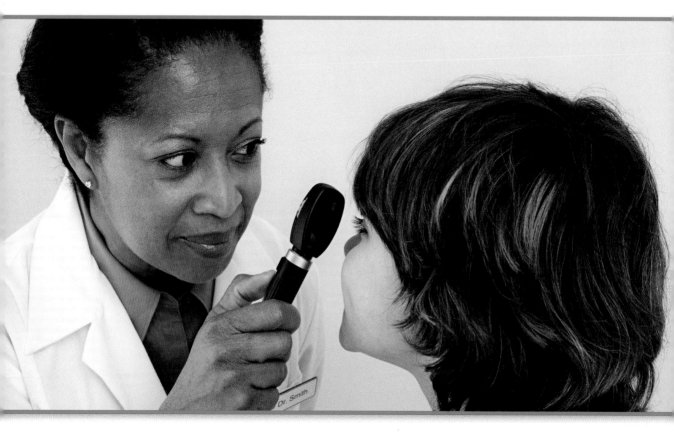

You may see a small flashlight used to shine a bright light at your eye.

You may also see a big machine that you have to sit near.

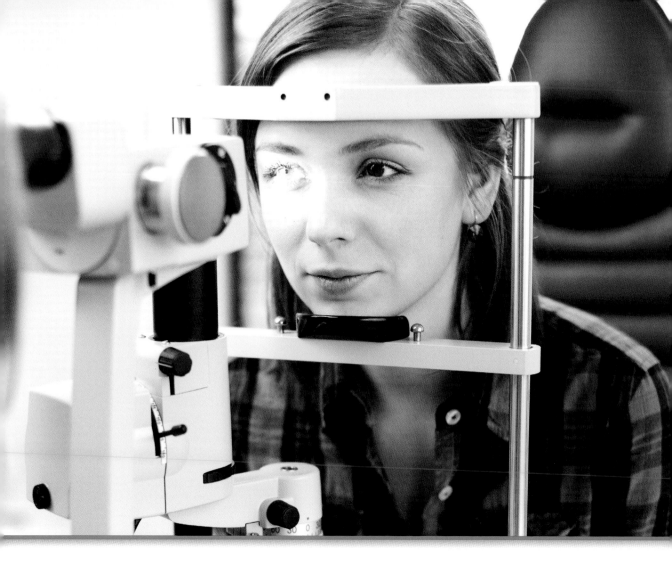

The eye **expert** uses both of these to look inside your eyes.

This helps him or her find out if you need to wear glasses.

Will I Need to Wear Glasses?

If an eye test shows that you have a problem, you might need to wear glasses.

There are lots of frames to choose from.

Glasses may help you see things close up or far away.

They can also help if one eye does not see as well as the other one.

What Other Help May I Get for My Sight?

If you need more help with your sight, then sometimes other tests are done.

You may go to a hospital to have these tests.

Some people find that one eye is weaker than the other.

Sometimes wearing an **eye patch** for a while can help to make it stronger.

Will the Eye Test Hurt?

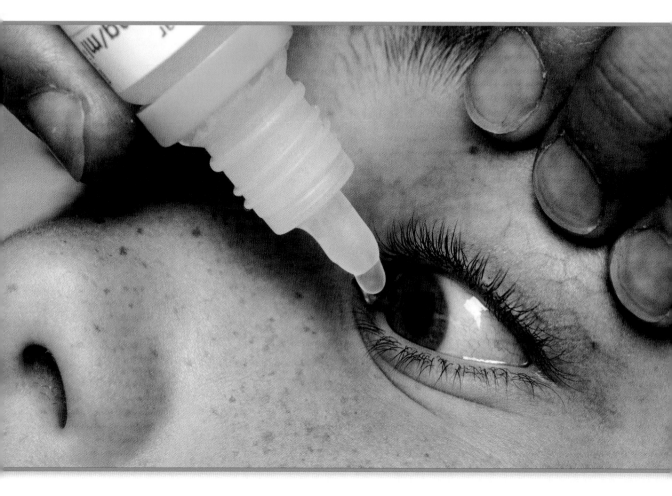

Some parts of your eye test may be uncomfortable. For example, if you need **eye drops**, it can feel strange.

But nothing during an eye test will hurt.

It is natural to feel a little nervous about your eye test.

But everything the eye **expert** does is to help you.

Tips to Keep Your Eyes Healthy

Dos:

✓ Do eat plenty of fruits and vegetables.

✓ Do wear sunglasses in bright light.

✓ Do rinse your eyes with water if you get dirt or dust in them.

Don'ts:

✗ Don't stick things into your eyes.

✗ Don't sit too close or for too long at the computer or television.

✗ Don't rub your eyes.

Picture Glossary

 **expert** someone who knows a lot about something and has special skills in that area

 **eye drops** special medicine for your eyes

 **eye patch** bandage or piece of cloth worn over one eye

 **lense** see-through piece of glass that you can look through to help you see things either close up or far away

optometrist someone who tests your eyesight

3 1308 00293 4263

Find Out More

Books

Dooley, Virginia. *I Need Glasses: My Visit to the Optometrist.* New York: Mondo, 2002.

Giles, Jenny, and Glenn Reynolds. *The Optometrist* (The Senses). Austin, Tex.: Harcourt Achieve, 2006.

Royston, Angela. *Healthy Eyes and Ears* (Look After Yourself). Chicago: Heinemann Library, 2003.

Websites

Learn more about eyesight and eyes at:
http://kidshealth.org/kid/stay_healthy/body/glasses.html

Discover more about your amazing eyes at:
http://kidshealth.org/kid/cancer_center/HTBW/eyes.html#

Index